fabulae

CRAB ORCHARD AWARD SERIES IN POETRY

fabulae

JOY KATZ

Crab Orchard Review

& Southern Illinois University Press

CARBONDALE AND EDWARDSVILLE

Printed in the United States of America

05 04 03 02   4 3 2 1

The Crab Orchard Award Series in Poetry is a joint publishing venture of Southern Illinois University Press and *Crab Orchard Review*. This series has been made possible by the generous support of the Office of the President of Southern Illinois University and the Office of the Vice Chancellor for Academic Affairs and Provost at Southern Illinois University Carbondale.

Crab Orchard Award Series in Poetry Editor: Jon Tribble
Judge for 2001: Maura Stanton

Library of Congress Cataloging-in-Publication Data
Katz, Joy, [date]
  Fabulae / Joy Katz.
    p. cm.—(Crab Orchard award series in poetry)
  I. Title. II. Series.
PS3611.A79 F33 2002
811'.6 — dc21
ISBN 0-8093-2444-X (pbk. : alk. paper)   2001047840

The paper used in this publication meets the minimum requirements of American National Standard for Information Sciences—Permanence of Paper for Printed Library Materials, ANSI Z39.48-1992. ♾

For my family

and for friends

Contents

TO A FALSE GOD

Acknowledgments

Grateful acknowledgment is made to the editors of the following journals in which poems in this collection first appeared, sometimes in slightly different form:

Antioch Review—"Falling"
Barrow Street—"Note Found Inside a Mezuzah"
Bellingham Review—"A Nation So Ignorant of Itself," "Still Life"
Boomerang—"Some Rain"
Boulevard—"In the Old Jewish Cemetery, Prague"
Chelsea—"Colophon," "Following the Orthodox Men"
Crab Orchard Review—"24th and Mission"
Delmar—"Sunday morning and the light"
The Fiddlehead—"Concerning the Islands Newly Discovered," "What Remains"
Laurel Review—"On Wardman Road," "Four Storeys"
LIT—"O How Unlike the Place from Whence They Fell"
The Minnesota Review—"You eat with your fingers"
Parnassus: Poetry in Review—"Taxonomy"
Pleiades—"Women Must Put Off Their Rich Apparel," "The Old Woman's Delight," "From the Water," "After John Taggart"
Quarter After Eight—"Falling Toward the Furnace"
Quarterly West—"The Imperfect Is Our Paradise"
Rain City Review—"The Entrance"
River City—"From the Forest of Canes"
Southwest Review—"From That Tree, You Must Not Eat"

"Women Must Put Off Their Rich Apparel," "The Imperfect Is Our Paradise," "Falling," "Concerning the Islands Newly Discovered," and "Taxonomy" also appear in the anthology *The New Young American Poets,* edited by Kevin Prufer (Southern Illinois University Press, 2000).

This work could not have been completed without the support of the Wallace Stegner Fellowship in Creative Writing at Stanford University, The MacDowell Colony, and Blue Mountain Center. Sincere gratitude to my teachers and to all whose encouragement and friendship helped this book along, including Robert Hass, Forrest Gander, Stanley Elkin, Naomi Lebowitz, Herbert Leibowitz, Kevin Prufer, Douglas Sanders, and Michael Wurster. Special thanks to Molly Peacock for her generous attention to this project. Thank you, Rob Handel.

following

the orthodox men

Women Must Put Off Their Rich Apparel

Women must put off their rich apparel;
at midday they must disrobe.

Apart from men are the folds of sleep,
daylight's frank remarks: the skin

of the eye, softening, softening.
Women must put on plainness,

the sweet set of the mouth's line;
the body must surface, the light,

the muscled indifference of deer.
A woman must let love recede,

the carved-out ribs sleep,
the vessel marked in bird lines

empty, as the sea empties her.
Say the sea, sound of leaves, the old

devotion, the call and response.
Reeds, caves, shoulders of cypress,

the woman who at this moment
does not need the world.

Following the Orthodox Men

through the diamond district, their black-suited, shoulder-to-shoulder lines
moving like script through the packed streets, past rubies and corals
polished as girls' knees, into bare metallic offices where they,
the Orthodox men, in their morning coats and white shirts
are the buyers and sellers of diamonds
and diamonds only, offerings of the earth as odorless as prayer,
diamonds sifting into the creases of white paper, coarse and crystalline as the salt
that drains the blood from meat and purifies it—and if I could belong
to the Orthodox men, if my body were modestly draped with linen,
my eyes cast down and my neck curved as the nail clippings
my grandfather wrapped and blessed and tossed into the stove
on Fridays—cuttings of the body made sacred—but I didn't choose
to be cut off from them and their God forever, or maybe
I did, from the moment I, as a girl, drew God—
who is never permitted to be drawn—with wild hair the color of sapphire.

From the Forest of Canes

Precious Consort T'ien, Kiangsai, 1931

Kingfisher Treasure let out her feet
a little each night until her lotus hooks,
slung like new moons, her perfect bean toes,
went flat as doors. My sway-hipped
cousin with the precious feet—gone. One less line
of doe-prints in the raked stone.

~

I am not Bound Branch Lotus with her bent body.
I am not Morning Lotus who walks on her heels,
nor Buddha's Head Lotus, hunched like the knot
on top of Sakyamuni's head, nor any other sigh.
I am Tsu Zhang's Fruit of June, the arch of my foot
doubled into itself, deep as a coin-purse.
Four toes broken and bound beneath—buried
like caterpillar-heads.

I bit the writing brush, prayed to the roe-deer moon
for these three-inch feet of a deer.
Now by decree I must let them out—
and let the blood, unbound, drill back into my toes.
I am to bring forth again the pain of binding.

~

I have not seen my feet since my fifth year.
This excites me.
My maid binds me weekly, her touch excites me;
we who cannot walk
grow fat until our sex is sixteen gates, one after another.
I have feet soft and round
as the dumplings whose water I drank for luck
the day I was bound.

There are men who drink our foot-washing water,
who put our golden feet into their mouths,
gathering radishes. Men who steal our red shoes
to sleep with on their journeys.
Let them try and rest without the scent of our feet,
watermelon seeds and almonds placed between the toes.

~

"How lucky to get a Cantonese wife! A face like jade,
large feet like an immortal's!"
I would rather be severed. Let them cut off my feet
for the mound in the square—
The "peak of golden lotuses!"
Let them nail me by my wound toes to a log. That will be
another kind of fulfillment.
I am still asked for, our devotees are here,
even those among the Party, whom Tsu Zhang bribes
into the many gift-box rooms of this place.

~

Desire is the foot with all the beauty of the body:
arched like the eyebrow,
round like the breast,
white like the face.

I will be fulfilled in dying, which will be for me a shout.

Desire returns in their dreams of our lotus hooks,
their dreams of us while we are yet dead or walking about
upon the flat lotus boats of country women.

Concerning the Islands Newly Discovered

Your Magnificent Lord,
having known the continual struggle
man undergoes
in praiseworthy new lands . . .

The good harbor, amaranth, trees like our willows
which drag the curve of cove like women's hair
falling

—The women especially,

                    their long black hair
            which makes them beautiful

It matters little to them if their appetite comes at midnight

The women are of noble body and we gave them
some of our things such as bells,
mirrors, glass beads

We took from them many things
        more praiseworthy and enduring

though of little value

Well may Your Magnificence forgive me
if I desire to remain—

if, nightly
alone in the ship's hold
I dig my hands into barrels of bells, glass beads,
mirrors, as if I am swimming . . .

Taxonomy

Language is only an instrument for the attainment of science,
Jefferson wrote Marbois
among the columns of names—
Senna, snake-root, lupine, Cherokee plum.
At Poplar Forest, he planted rows of scaly bark hickory,
measured fisted buds of poke.

∼

Random strokes and knots, scribbles
of hair on the crushed, sweat-drenched linen
of his wife's pillow as she lay dying.
Present occupations disable me from completing
the Notes, he wrote. His fine fingers
brushed dovetailed corners of coffin—
his infant daughter's. Outside,
jasmine and wethawk in the marbled cold
of spring sky.
              Royston crow, towhee,
and the sting of Tarleton in the wide, shallow mouths
of common salt near Monticello.

∼

Nights he walked ragged, trampled rows
of cabbage to the line of small shacks, yellow oil
lamplight, a neighborhood of slaves.
The spirit of the master is abating.

∼

You can stand on a cliff before the heave and tear
in Jefferson's mountains, in the sublime,
and not escape the awe. You can kneel above the abyss,
two hundred and seventy feet
of gouged rock, your back to silver grilles

of cars parked row on row in sun.
Here the eye ultimately composes itself,
Jefferson added later, much later—looking away to the plain,
away from the arch that sprung
as it were, up to heaven.

A Nation So Ignorant of Itself

John Wesley Powell in the Grand Canyon, 1869

He came into the canyon with nine men,
a keg of whiskey, a copy of King Lear.
Eight hundred feet of black gneiss, eight hundred feet
of quartzites, exceedingly hard,
ringing under the hammer.
Late May: the air wavered, silt-filled;
from the piñons, a sound strangely like the sea.

~

At dusk Powell would go off and scale the cliffs;
he measured walls; he would jam
his single arm into a crack.
Finding I am caught here
four hundred feet above the river . . .
Trapped, helpless,
he praised the sky.

~

What he must have told his wife —
Massive ferns
enamelled stalks and maiden hair
covering the rocks about the falls
What is it like to live with someone
who has seen this kind of beauty?
The boat leapt
like a deer in the woods . . .
Touching someone who has seen
a wall of diamonds

~

and what could he keep of that place?
Springs wind like silver threads along the sand.
Did the images fade like the feeling in his lost arm?
The explorer's life is wasted,
said Meriwether Lewis
and shot himself at Grinder's Inn.

⁓

But a nation came west
to the foreign part of itself,
past salients and cracked schist and clouds
that skimmed the gorges, past lichened sandstone,
pinnacles, red rock liquefying at sunset,
past the homes of old arrow-makers,
and made its life.

We have little time to spend in admiration,
so on we go.

Some Rain

Freud saw his first patient on a gray morning in Vienna;
cobblestones glistened feebly.
And it was pouring as Pollock dragged red onto *Full Fathom Five*.
Patty Hearst's face was grainy and soft, on closed-circuit,
as if we were watching her through a wet screen door,
but Socrates, as he died, looked sharply into the distance.
Early evening. Water coursed the gutters.
Remember the morning after, when Benjamin Franklin
did nothing in particular?
And how light loved the wipers on the bus to Selma?
Showers ruffled the Potomac as the burglars
were led over the Watergate lawn;
you could hear horses plashing as Galileo upended his telescope
to peer at the enormous, hairy legs of a housefly.
Watson, come here, I need you. Drops clung to the railings,
ran over the roof in thin streams.
In a soaking mist, the *Lusitania* gently sank;
bicycles stood in the rain as the students left Tiananmen Square.
The Lindbergh baby vanished through a wet, streaked window.
A few pale-green leaves were stuck to it.
Jane Eyre came back to find Rochester fumbling in a storm,
the yard full of fallen branches.
The tulip market crashed during a terrible downpour,
but oxen grazed patiently at Lascaux, not minding.
If, as Hitler was declared chancellor, the crowd opened its umbrellas,
people stood barefoot in the mud sometimes at Birkenau.
The banality of evil, Hannah Arendt wrote, crushed out her cigarette,
and got up to shut the windows.
As Marie Curie set out a small, glowing dish of radium
with her poisoned fingers, a line of storms was moving east;
faintly it thundered while my grandparents listened,
for the first time, to a phonograph.
Lewis Carroll wrote Alice onto the riverbank
while he floated downstream. The first drops were falling;
it was cool and still as the morning Alaric sacked Rome
or the one—it was June—Dickinson looked out at the grass
and said—something. What? Now that was some rain.

the word wife

On Wardman Road

Pillbugs clench under the cracked slate of the garden.
Massive clippers: their *whisk*— *snip*
heavy in the slowing repetitions of August.
The child in the tiger lilies looks up.
One silence is the shuddering ladder; another,
the father's white, unfamiliar muscles
against the dark hedge.

⁓

Tame light, the apparition of driveways.
Soft brown, milky white, yellow garages;
neat perimeters, backyards.
What's missing is the violent perfection of shadows,
and I mentally paint them in—shadows
from the skinny poplars, inert cars.

⁓

At bedtime the child,
thinking of the father's muscles, asks
could you kill me? —*no.*
I mean, could you choke me, could
you squeeze me so hard that I would die?
He senses that his yes is necessary
for her to be sure of him, and his *yes* is brief,
face flickering with something.
He pulls the blanket to her chin
before brushing a strand of hair from her forehead
and leaving the room.
The open windows are two wide eyes
flat against the mild dark.

⁓

The child is forbidden the second door
of her bedroom, which opens to the porch roof.
Sometimes she walks out, asphalt shingles
waving unevenly under bare feet. If it is evening,
the heat from the roof rises slowly up her legs
in the cool air. She stays close to the door,
close to the breath of the house.

From the Water

The mother's belly is deeply tanned. A belief—that this is the last attractive part of her body—floats loosely above the rest of her thoughts, the way the lit, flashing water in the pool floats above the depths. Her younger daughter is sleek as a gill. The older is less angular, softening, the way sharp edges of just-plowed snow begin to soften in wind. The girls rise one behind the other, splashing and laughing, from the ladder. They lie face down on hot cement, talking more softly as they warm, and as they warm they move from spot to spot. Their suits leave rows of dark torso-shapes behind, which fade slowly in the sun as their mother gets up and moves toward them from her chair on the grass.

Falling

1. PROSERPINA

She got pulled down and learned to like it. It happened gradually, from the warmth maybe, the moans . . . all those half-years in hell and one day a murmur, almost somnolent, *all right then, fuck me in the ass.*

This was the day she returned, bloodied and dreamy, one broken heel and dress inside out, to the frozen earth—the first time spring came late. Ceres knew then she had lost her. Blanched almonds and fennel, boiled wheat, white seeds, offerings for the dead; Ceres bit her fingerpads until they burst like grapes.

2. HEROIN

What would happen, they said, is that we would like it, and then we would do anything for it. The drug seemed like chalk dust or powdered orchids, and I dreamed at night about the needle:

Dragonfly metal and a barrel like clouds, plunger pushing waves of liquid like melted nacre. It would feel like clouds, I imagined—"opiate," opaline slipping-down feeling of sleep coming on. They would push the tine into the nearly-finned skin between my toes, the tiny veins—

I ran into my mother's bed, clenched my legs to my chest, clenched my feet into my hands, and lay awake all night sweating and cleaving. I would like it. I would like it like heaven and would be lost.

Abraham Considers

The snail-shaped hollow in Isaac's neck,
slight curve he strokes, singing *sleep,*
sleep. The neck pale as a new lamb;
the lambs in the hands of the *shochet,* each
with its clean cut, dropping silently, as into sleep.
The heads of flowers, nodding unbearably.
Winestems that snap in the hand;
the necks of spoons, thin as sandal-straps;
·the straps that bind
Isaac's uninjurable neck. The knife
drawn back, sure and sturdy. *God, god,*
Abraham throws back his head
and laughs.

Four Storeys

You can pluck up the roof with your fingernails. Underneath it, in the attic story, a boy at a white enameled desk operates a ham radio. When I lift the attic and set it gently into my palm, he doesn't notice, going on with his *da-di-das*. I place the attic on the ground, and he climbs out the window and walks off to see if the rest of the street has changed.

The second story, with its darkened bedrooms, is empty save for the sleep-ing mother—and comes up too easily, like a glass pitcher that turns out to be plastic.

Meanwhile, the sudden wind in the living room lifts the sheet music from its stand and pulls it into an airborne *s*. The young woman at the viola scowls. I have interrupted her practice. She flings her bow onto a chair. In the kitchen, the cabinet doors are blowing open and shut. Since this is the kitchen story, you can unscrew it like a jar and lay it aside.

In the basement, four small girls call "*morn-*ing!" because, having stretched out and closed their eyes for a moment to mark the passage of night, it is morning. After a second they realize the cellar's brightness is real; they squint upward, hair flying into their faces. I'll tell you what none of them know: I buried a piece of coal under the foundation so that I will come back when I'm old, dig up the diamond, and be rich.

Handwork

for K. G.

It is an evening in late spring. Her husband died some years ago. She leaves the task of dinner dishes—pleasant smell of mud and grass from the kitchen window, hands in warm water—to get the tent for a weekend trip. It is underneath the basement steps, still folded from the last time he packed it away: many flat, neat rectangles, tight as a map. She takes the tent into her hands, surprised at its solid weight. Then she stands up and shakes it out. The tent seems to float for a moment before settling to the floor. She is crying. It was the last she had of his body in the house, and she has undone it.

Nuptial

for Beatrice Rabinovitz

She has forgotten her life, so we don't speak much.
I am content to sit with her
but on this day cannot enter the room—light
rises around her in layers, makes an antechamber—
as if I have stumbled upon a bride.
There is the intimacy of skull, round
beneath her silver hair. The chair
where she rests her twisted fingers
is carved with flowers.
On the dresser, double frame:
a photograph of her face, and one of Tom's,
after the wedding. Their eyes aren't afraid: they gaze
ahead, as she does now into the mirror.
Morning has pressed the linen shirt to my back,
making it finely creased, soft,
like the skin of her hand.
This is the giving away—
not later, when I will receive her ring; later
she will be ritually bathed, then the winding
immaculate sheet.

Solstice

There is a night in summer, a girl with braces on her teeth.
There is the lengthening of darkened hours, a

gradation not quite the desire for sleep—
she knows the feeling is more quiet, like running

her fingers down the inside of her arm.
It comes from the place where her hair is gently braided

and unbraided, brushed against her neck
by unnamed hands. She wears soft things, a skirt that falls

against her calf; she says *kiss* into the mirror,
sees the distance between the word and its reflection.

Through the window, evening light; next door,
Japanese lanterns, pink and uneven in the dark.

A Visit to Seattle

Leaves falling in mild air, November. Black-eyed Susans gone
except for their dead centers—a cloud of small entrances
into night. The corner of a lake, and afternoon light ending;
deep water spreading to indigo.
The distance between you is the floor of a room
that is empty, and terribly bright.

~

Gloved hellos: the bed against an outside wall that's always cold,
making love with harbor lights outside. Harbor lights?
He asks *have you ever been with a stranger*
and you, thinking *not until this moment*—

~

Sudden lightness as his weight lifts from bed. Your sleep
has been as shallow as the sound of dresser drawers opening.
Coffee, too ubiquitous to reassure, in a kitchen
with open shelves—every thing revealed. Earthenware,
blue and brown glaze, is a heaviness in your hands
belonging to this house.

~

He says, driving, *I love all this boat stuff* meaning the pilings,
houseboats, boatyards with the long barges, gangways.
You think of kayaking alone into the Sound,
the scale of your body against ships' hulls, the way
you might pass over the surface between them
like a delicate insect.

~

He is washing windows outside. Inside,
streams of water seem to cling to your reflected face
and the sun cuts your arms in hard shapes.
Sheets that smelled like skin, torn from the bed,
hang like clean bandages on the line.

Falling Toward the Furnace

We are painting the dining room of our new house and have removed the register covers. The cats wander into the air ducts. They roam the interior and complex systems, learning parts of the house I will never know in a thousand mornings of stumbling downstairs for coffee. So far they come back, but I'm afraid one is falling toward the furnace.

Once I made a dress and threw it away when it was done. I knew all its linings and seams, had cut and fit and touched each part. Its red silk seemed to throw off a slight heat like the fat, freckled body of the boy who sat next to me in homeroom that year shifting his knees back and forth, back and forth.

The power goes out. I think of my heart and lungs, worry that these parts will falter if brought to consciousness. I'm groping the hallway. The skull under my scalp is one brief beam thrown from a passing car.

What keeps coming back is that I have so many tasks to accomplish that I begin before the walls have taken hold. I run down half-formed hallways calling *wait, let me touch you*. The light switch is black, a moving stain in darkness, but I flip it and hold up my hand. Light comes back, bleeds through the skin: bright aureole of each finger, red bone shadows, smooth.

Tour Book of Northeastern States

for M. D.

To pass nothing but low shrub and pasture,
traveling a route traced in yellow by a girl who said,
helpfully, *this way.* There is no religion.
The pines are neither sickly nor ecstatic;
there is nothing beyond what the roadside offers,
miles ticked out in green. Fire Island
is not filled with men, one of them so sick with grief
he fucks one lover after another, trying to die.
If you want to rest, there are rest stops.
There are neat paragraphs of beach—you can go there
the way I wanted to get hit by a car when my friend died,
not thinking I deserved pain, but
to hurt myself in rage, so the body could howl with all of itself.
The tour book is not full of promise,
just motels, clean campsites, paths to the dunes.
Someone else is driving and throws a blanket back
over you, in the cold evening air.
Sleep pulls you down;
it is a sweet place the body is going.

Sunday morning and the light

slips through the blinds in crazy zebra patterns
she believes, for an instant, are attached to their bodies—
lazy, playing, she moves the now-unfamiliar
angle of her elbow back and forth among the shadows.
What happened with his grandfather:
*I remember we sucked each other's penises. I remember
liking it,* he says simply.   A six-year-old boy,
the fabric of his pants eased off the light skin
of his belly. She can't see the man's face, just hands
reaching for the child's waist. *When did it turn,
when did it turn from pleasure?*
He says nothing
                    as a breeze
pulls the blind to the window-frame and lofts it out again;
church bells through the window,
a hymn in hollow alto chimes all out of tune.
Why did you ask what happened with my grandfather?
—*Because it's a part of you,*
she offers after a moment, having nothing to offer
but this: the time she found a single egg,
cream-brown shell against pale earth, still warm.
She could not touch it without knowing it had come
through the body of some living thing,
and somehow still belonged to that.
She wanted to drop the egg
and at the same time stand very still and hold it until
it became something light,
as much a part of herself as breathing.

The Word Wife

When the silence between them
was a new thing—a morning in a garden—
he took a pencil and sketched her feet.
He matched her ankles
in crisp lines falling like wisps
of hair from a boy's first cut.
The quick strokes were moths
lighting her body, the background
white, like the word *wife,* first light
touching the violet's hair. The new word
husband, hush of a car up the street.
Pigeons swallowing their tongues beneath the eaves.

Aubade

　　　　　　—but I rose and the day
passed and it was dark when I walked the hallway
and found you, already asleep, turned from me
like an accidental photo—odd angle of sky,
a thumb, that minute
I decided to keep, and kept, but forgot. The back
of your head on its pillow, a gentle, intimate shape—
it was something, it was eternal.

Lullaby, Four A.M.

To come out of hiding, little turnip-mouth, clouds among.
Dawn's here, wind on the floor; the big tureen moon
spills its pale soup of stars.
Potatoes and books in their jackets. The fridge shivers off.

I want to hear the sun's old story.
I want to be warmed and made to listen.
I want to be chased and spooned up like a drop of mercury.

The names curl off their place cards, stretch and say *who?*
And you, soft as a fruit, little keychain-eyes: *who?*
The planets rest in their bead-strings, the seeds in their flower-faces.
And the trees lisp and the glass greens.

The Old Woman's Delight

after Baudelaire

Everyone wished to please the little boy on his birthday;
everyone imagined his serious smile
except the silver-haired old woman who, laying out his gift,
said, "I hope he tells me *I don't like this toy.*"
"Yes," she went on, tapping the box shut and smiling
as what she imagined took hold: "That would be fine with me!
Grandma I don't like this." The little boy,
dark-eyed and white-sneakered like her, the old woman,
but in fact quite unlike herself, quite apart from herself.
She joyed at this
the way a mother is glad of an infant's lusty kick
away. This old woman, with her crooked violets
and orange hatbox, is glad the age of pleasing is past.

Café

A downpour has ended and now the peaceful,
steady kind of light that's after,
little spits of rain left in the wind still.
                              A child,
crying and crying hysterically, until he is shuddering
convulsively, leaves off, and when this happens
the same feeling of steadiness. He sits across from his mother,
shivering every now and then.
In a minute he will return to his drawing.

If you are with someone who does not say anything to you,
who does not touch you or ask anything of you
but goes on sitting across from you and after a time
goes back to her book, that's grace.
                              It returns the world
already in progress: steaming milk, opening newspapers.
And a man walks in carrying a birdcage.

together in a small room

In the Old Jewish Cemetery, Prague

The dead here, impacted in their ascent
like molars in a small jaw,
                and the living
who skit about in the bone light
      of trying to say something to them
and to each other—
              effaced of name, broken, jammed-in,
the headstones after all say nothing;
        they bite into the footpath,
            a bad perforation between worlds.

    We leave pebbles
on this heave of graves, leave stones that are like boils
         or the heads of tacks
or bells to charm the natives
                stay down, stay down

I think the dead are not more holy.
                How do we know they
       in their inverted world trail stars for us?
I would say something irreverent about someone
buried here, if I knew her—
            I think the dead say nothing
anyway; it is too noisy with this din
of gray alphabet, this empty trail of thought balloon
and my own radioactive stone—
            a falsehood, an
embarrassment, dot of a question mark,
              something inarticulate
like a baby who cries out at night
      just to see if its own voice is there

Metamorphosis

The intermediate forms, the ones growing extra wings,
the first, accidental black moths, the mixed-up immigrant
tongues, what will they come to?
                              Consider this woman
playing bridge: she survived Dachau. Like a mermaid
she has not the right form for either world.
A talent for suffering;
a safe exile.

A capacity for suffering,

                    —dumb as child's hair,
dumb as the flowers and fruit they plant now
along the walls of Terezin . . .

This is not the opera glove
of a snake molting; the next form, hard,
muscled, is not visible—

                    I didn't get to die with the rest

What expands, enlarges,
to let the body live
has given her something like an extra
wing—
          her laughter at bridge scattering
like wings, her dead husband dragged after her,
useless wing—her life itself a kind of
extra wing?

Is it that she has grown everything she needs?

Or that a bomb has gone off
and she waiting all these years to hear the report

Together in a Small Room (1975)

All afternoon the "gestapo" called us upstairs to their demon bedrooms
and asked us why they should let us live.
They were our youth group leaders, a couple in their twenties.
I couldn't imagine being twenty, it was
like a room so far upstairs I couldn't see it.
They meant to teach us about the camps, they crowded us
together in a small room, but I was full of desire to live
which meant knowing something to say to the boy
beside me on the sofa. I loved him
like we were family to each other. I couldn't even get to that place.
Pretty soon I was sent off to be killed
with the others on the back porch—
Just what we need, a Jewish doctor, our leaders said
of the most useful thing I could think of, to be:
something I could imagine because I knew the steps, saw the way.

At Terezin (1992)

Standing in a solitary confinement cell, I think of how, traveling, I so easily grow accustomed to less. A window seat on a bus. A seat on a bus. A bus. A bed to myself. Some light. A cell with a window. I almost cry in the cell, feeling foolish, crying because I am supposed to but beginning to see how they left their homes behind. Until this moment, I had thought—I would have said *shoot me in my house;* I would never have come here.

What Remains

We are at Terezin, walking among what remains. Beatrice is with us.

   She is dead already, but I worry for her; so fragile, to imagine this place

would have killed her. Jacek is with us—a Pole, a Catholic. It is Terezin,

   but all the ruins are here. Belzec, Sobibor, the death places marked

in bright outlines: Jacek on his knees, saying Kaddish for them all.

   There is still ash on the ground. Ash in the wind. I let it fall on my arms

and my face—the way, if I took care of someone hurt, I wouldn't mind

   about the blood. Beatrice is frightened and angry to be here, wandering

as if punished, like the spirit of the dead Levite. I must say Kaddish

   so that she can stay dead. I begin over and over, *Magnified and sanctified,*

but the lines get tangled. I forget it's not a death poem, that it's praise—

The Entrance

Yet, here is a way into the poem:
It is as if I have drawn, on watercolor paper, the entrance
to a well. I have drawn a whole landscape, in fact,
for the poem to take place:
hills in the distance, curving toward water.

In the foreground are a few objects:
a jack, a domino, three marbles. They lie very close to the edge.

Do not step too near the hole I have drawn—
there is no fence around it.
I made it, but even I cannot approach;
I could step accidentally in, and it is depthless.

Look how close the child's toys are to the edge of the well.
Look how dark the opening is. Am I lying?
Did I draw this landscape? The entrance
can't be mine—

It was drawn by a gypsy girl whose hair I have always envied.
She exists; I am not even making her up.
She wears cloaks and shoes with pointed toes,
and she cries over dinner, in front of the drawing.
See the tears in her eyes as she describes her father,
the stories he read to her in Russian
when she was a girl. She has drawn this hole, which is just
wide enough for her body to fall, straight down.

Maybe I am the older sister. Who can say why I am trapped
here in this landscape? Every rock I pick up is round and white,
slightly irregular, like the hills—featureless.
There is nowhere for me to go
but to face the entrance into the ground—and you,
reader, can you get out of the poem?
By not finishing, by turning the page?

to a false god

24th and Mission

A girl finishing her fried chicken lets it fall,
skin and haunches and razored wings
and coleslaw, a lavish drop—the glory of it—
easily as a child lets a stick go, as the hair pulls from the head
of the dying man, who wants to know
have we been saved? Cups and glass and private trash,
Q-tips in the cracks of pavement: the tide of us rising, skimmed off.
Chocolate-milk cartons, diapers, and—a little more fun—
onion rings and fried rice from the Chinese/donut shop.
And the frank, soily excess of the shoe-shine men: their rank, their talk.
(To be saved, scraped clean, empty as the sound of gulls!)
I work my way through our kingdom, past squalls
of flowers, rutted plantains, burst tomatoes,
to the panedería, for slabs of sugared bread: take and eat
and throw some down. The ground with its load of food,
doves in their marvelous robes—the sun goes all golden,
softened. And the dying man cries out
at 24th and Mission, *Repent!*

You eat with your fingers

leave the bones like a watch all taken apart

Even your mother
color of the city messed over her hands
takes food from your fingers
                              kissing them

River women dunk their babies in a flash
and catch them up like fish

I love
how slowly you eat

You put your fingers into rice freely
You put your hand into the warm mouths of sleepers

You push the tiny bones from the linen
of the fish skin
hold the flesh out to my lips
                              as for a child

Photograph of Plath

Because her lips are parted roughly,
shaped like a scream, I want to turn away for a second

as if she were the young girl burned by napalm.
But I know she isn't suffering, only speaking.

So I look, the way I looked through *The Bell Jar*
for words that pointed somewhere you can't get back from.

When I crossed the border to that other country
myself, a woman said to me, very gently, *you walk like a foreigner.*

Is there anything hidden here, in her face?
(Snow-fields hoarding white owls)

I want to let it land on my sleeve
and let it fly back.

Emergency

I wake to a sound like cats purring,
bend the blinds and squint, a taste of metal.
Red lights, no sirens—
the house across the street is burning.
                              I had been dreaming
of an old woman whose eyes,
swollen and dried as nutshells, I soothed with oil.
Now the door of her house breathes cold air
and her poppies belong to anybody, so I picked them.
Who am I that they should open and cry out to me?

To a False God

My favorite scenes have the real life of black and white, a coarse grain handed down from newsreels, burned buildings, and *The Cabinet of Dr. Caligari*—Werner Krauss's sad lope, those drooped and sloping shoulders which, seen from the back, *are* sorrow, caved in like a dying lily, hollow and sweet like a trumpet. "That walk," said Krauss, "I put it on like an old coat." A trick then! Like the painted shadows, so I won't fail to find the real sadness in his small glances and gestures: felt emotions "of which," Krauss said, "I am not the master."

L'Arrivéê d'un Train en Gare

When the Lumiere brothers showed the first film
on the darkened café wall that was the first screen,
and the crowd watched their bodies, bright as bait,
dazzle into the sun, it was like the first time
I saw the queer tray-shape
that was my own face
                        turning toward the camera.

—And once, on a train through the flat Midwest,
a horizonful of clouds looked so exactly
like a splitting range of Alps,
I became another person, with another life.
This woman I was felt so strange and real
I wanted to push her off the seat,
like the train in *L'Arrivéê* that came speeding toward the audience—
they ran to the back of the room.

The girls touched their skirts and laughed. The men
talked loudly, watching their filmed hands flash
like fish in a bucket. "Modigliani,"

a man in front of my house said to me one day,
"you look like a woman in Modigliani.
I've been watching you from my room."

O How Unlike the Place from Whence They Fell

He is helplessly putting dishes into the drainer to the on and off
of Clooney's pub sign. She is on the sofa, where she sews and listens to opera:
toffee-colored buttons on a camel coat. She becomes aware it's taking her
one button per aria. Seven buttons left! Seven tragic deaths!
On his walk that afternoon, he'd found the perfect stride
to just hit the far side of each paving block. The satisfaction of it lingered all day,
so that he hardly worried when the strokes of her hairbrush
just failed to match the swipes of the gardener's rake.
"Let's go out for ice cream," he says. They are in the car when suddenly
he is speeding exactly as fast as the train alongside them,
as if it were the needle that would stitch them to the world.
"Home free!" he cries, running a red light. If she weren't counting cars
she might have seen it, bobbing over the empty intersection,
like fruit about to fall on its own.

From That Tree, You Must Not Eat

First, she imagined the taste.
She didn't mean to, but the fruit tormented her
with its colors of the world.
The snake said, everyone's eating it.
Look how happy they are.
She stopped eating
everything. She felt light as the rib of a new-made boat
and decided to keep the fruit around, in bowls.
It was so pretty, and she didn't even want it—
she didn't want anything; she felt light as the arm
of a crystal chandelier.
Adam said, you look beautiful. Let's play volleyball.
That night she couldn't sleep. In the kitchen,
in the dark, she choked down sixteen of the fruit
very fast and made herself throw up.
God said that didn't count.
She was happy; she felt light as the rib
of a plastic drinking straw. She looked almost translucent.
Is anything wrong? asked Adam. Is this breakfast?
Two slices of apple
on a bone-white plate.

The Imperfect Is Our Paradise

An orange leaf on every finger bowl: a dozen tongues,
mute about their clear water and their own orange scent

and the way the glass pressures the heavy, white-flossed linen
a little, as a cat flattens grass in the yard.

Suppose that this complete simplicity
is the torment itself, delighting nothing of the vital I?

The wainscoting smiles in refraction through the clear water;
the cone of the whelk catches the frank daylight

from the window, and so appears whiter than the white freesia
in its vase. I don't know how to live with beauty.

Even the held breath of expectation enlarges it—
places set for guests to sing and slap the table

until the silver jumps like fish from their boisterous grace.
When the walls were wet I loved their particular blue.

The height of the flowers through the door's arch
is another thing I can't escape—the trouble is the stillness,

the *not* desiring so much more than this: an orange leaf
on every finger bowl.

After John Taggart

A sound not quite brushes,
but still urging. Stiff-bristled broom-sweeps
steady as the broom hits plumb,
the concrete.
Small sift of dust under, slipping.
                                    Listen.
This thinnest ocean
of dust under the urge.

This must be heard. Not the urge of *the*
to which the world attends,
but this thinnest ocean,
swept under, over and left
behind on the ground.
This must be heard.

But I want the urge too. The insist.
I want the insist to push—you have to work,
to push hard, not to miss the underbreath of—

The urge is strong. The fingers grip the broom like vine.

Note Found Inside a Mezuzah

I left white lights in the plants,
a ziggurat of beachstones,
o mares eat oats and does eat oats
in child-scrawl next to the washer

and arrived here. Autumn emerged
from the bursting fig.

Someone before me tucked bits
of cork into the window frames
to stop the *yes no yes* of the glass.

Outside, planes glister and hang
like fruit over brick façades; I found
a cock ring in the cabinet.
Here are outsized crow-shadows
cast from the next-door roof.

The few leaves in the teacup's arch
say *answer, answer.*

At Nice, rows of naked bathers
like clothespins tacked at the shoreline.

Still Life

How things come to light as I draw them: the curved-wire stem
of that flower which, until my eye moved to the prill of dried petal
and past that to the dead sepal
and then down to the stalk, I didn't see.
I can draw that, *prill,* which is both the look and the sound
that piece would make, if it could, the way a thumbnail skimming comb tines
sings this small-spoked bunch of reeds.

⁓

An unfolded letter flying into a stack-spill of paper
is one of the movements of my house, like the flowers' upward flourish.
The book's deckle, rough like slate
makes the metal sound of water dripping
as the pencil dips and dips, marking its shadows.
What else must be happening in this room? I want to throw it all out

⁓

for one note, a leaf in the center of the floor.
But below the curve of the bottle neck, far at the table's edge,
the tubed-out whelk startles in its whiteness, reflecting
more light than it can possibly gain from dusk—
the phosphorescence of paper, but more pure,
and organic as skin
as though life were in it still.

It causes this sweet rolling forward,
like the crown of a shell: a gentle pressure to work.

Colophon

Just now the typographer's *a* comes into being.
Her hands have ached to shape its curves:
many strokes of black, then white, then again black, taking
a long time to dry in between: flawless,
the letter has always belonged to the world.

Typeface does not correspond to *a,* or *b,* or *c,* nor the shoulders of *m,*
nor the sweet hooks of lower-case *g*s, but to all the letterforms—
"The beauty that radiates from the work of men," said Eric Gill,
making the slope of the buttocks and shoulders and the small tight backs
of his lovers into the Gill Sans type that letters the London Underground,
"is the beauty of holiness." The typographer's *a,* now finished,

will be reproduced digitally and set into text columns,
sale circulars, billboards. If a word is elegy to what it signifies,
does *woman* disappear? Words say what they will against us,
but the serif of *a* hangs still as an earring. My body is here
at the end of *idea,* at the center of *eat, say, dance.*

"Women Must Put Off Their Rich Apparel": The first two lines are taken from Virginia Woolf's novel *Mrs. Dalloway*.

"Taxonomy": The italicized portions are taken from Thomas Jefferson's journal *Notes on the State of Virginia*.

"A Nation So Ignorant of Itself": John Wesley Powell lost his right arm in the Civil War. He eventually became head of both the U.S. Geological Survey and the Bureau of Ethnology. The italicized portions of this poem are taken from his journal *The Exploration of the Colorado River and Its Canyons*. The book's introduction quotes Samuel Bowles, editor of the Springfield (Massachusetts) *Republican* and an admirer of Powell, who wrote in 1868 of the then-uncharted Colorado River country: "Is any other nation so ignorant of itself?"

"The Old Woman's Delight": The title refers to Charles Baudelaire's poem "The Old Woman's Despair" from *Paris Spleen*.

"Abraham Considers": Translated from the Hebrew, Isaac's name literally means "he laughs." A *shochet* is a ritual slaughterer.

"The Imperfect Is Our Paradise": This poem is in conversation with Wallace Stevens's "The Poems of Our Climate" from *The Palm at the End of the Mind*.

CRAB ORCHARD AWARD SERIES IN POETRY

Muse
Susan Aizenberg

This Country of Mothers
Julianna Baggott

In Search of the Great Dead
Richard Cecil

Names above Houses
Oliver de la Paz

The Star-Spangled Banner
Denise Duhamel

Winter Amnesties
Elton Glaser

Train to Agra
Vandana Khanna

Crossroads and Unholy Water
Marilene Phipps

Misery Prefigured
J. Allyn Rosser